Leo Brouwer

Un Dia de Noviembre

for guitar

Chester Music

UN DIA DE NOVIEMBRE

for Guitar

LEO BROUWER

Andante cantabile

D.C. fino a 𝄋 e subito a Fine

LEO BROUWER

Composer, guitarist and music director, Leo Brouwer was born in Havana, in 1939. He studied with I. Nicola, Pujol's pupil and specialising in composition, completed his studies at the Juilliard School of Music and at Hartt School, University of Hartford.

In 1987 Brouwer was selected, along with Isaac Stern and Alan Danielou, honourable member of UNESCO in recognition for his music career. He has conducted orchestras around the world, including the Berlin Philharmonic, the Scottish National, the BBC Concert and the Mexico National Symphony Orchestra. He has been heard as both composer and classical guitarist at many major international music events and his *Cancion de Gesta* (Epic Poem) has been performed by orchestras throughout the world.

His discography comprises over a hundred commercial recordings and his works have been recorded by John Williams, Julian Bream, Franz Bruggen and Harry Sparnay as well as The Toronto Festival, the London Sinfonietta and the Liège Festival.

Brouwer has also written many film scores, including *A Walk in the Clouds* and Alfonso Arau's internationally acclaimed *Like Water for Chocolate*.

Brouwer is General Manager of the Cuban National Symphony Orchestra and, since 1992, has conducted the Córdoba Orchestra in Spain. In 1998, he was awarded the Manuel de Falla Prize and in 1999, the National Music Prize for Cuba.